TOWER HAMLETS PUBLIC LIBRARY

C001277

KT-566-736

The Canterbury Tales

G

Series

idea

Library Learning Information

Idea Store® Bow
1 Gladstone Place
Roman Road
London E3 5ES

020 7364 4332

Created and managed by
Tower Hamlets Council

Pearson Education Limited
Edinburgh Gate, Harlow,
Essex CM20 2JE, England
and Associated Companies throughout the world.

ISBN-13: 978-0-582-42114-1
ISBN-10: 0-582-42114-4

This edition first published 2000

5 7 9 10 8 6

Copyright © Penguin Books Ltd 2000
Illustrations by Victor Ambrus
Opening illustration by David Cuzik (Pennant Illustration)
Cover design by Bender Richardson White

Typeset by Pantek Arts Ltd, Maidstone, Kent
Set in 11/14pt Bembo
Printed in China
SWTC/05

*All rights reserved; no part of this publication may be reproduced, stored
in a retrieval system, or transmitted in any form or by any means,
electronic, mechanical, photocopying, recording or otherwise, without the
prior written permission of the Publishers.*

Published by Pearson Education Limited in association with
Penguin Books Ltd, both companies being subsidiaries of Pearson Plc

For a complete list of titles available in the Penguin Readers series, please write to your local
Pearson Education office or to: Penguin Readers Marketing Department,
Pearson Education, Edinburgh Gate, Harlow, Essex CM20 2JE.

Contents

Tower Hamlets	
Suppliers Code	AVA
Price	£4.30
Invoice Date	01/11/2006
LOC	BOW
Class	428.6
Barcode	C001277031

Introduction

'As you know, it's a long way to Canterbury. You need to stay happy on the journey. I've got an idea. You must all tell a story on the way. We'll give a free dinner to the person who tells the best story. Now, put up your hands if you agree.'

The pilgrims all held up their hands and cried out, 'Yes!'

A group of pilgrims are travelling together for five days from London to Canterbury. On the way, each pilgrim has to tell a story. Some stories are happy, and some are sad. But they all have a message, and we can learn from them.

The writer of these tales, Geoffrey Chaucer, was born in London in about 1342. We do not know exactly when he was born. His father, John, and his grandfather, Robert, worked in the wine business. They probably also worked for King Edward III. The family earned quite a lot of money and had a comfortable life.

When he was a young boy, Chaucer went to school in London. He then worked for an important lady in the king's family. It was a very good job and he met some very interesting people.

In 1359 Chaucer was sent abroad as a soldier. He was fighting for the king against France in part of the Hundred Years' War. He was taken prisoner by the French near Rheims, but after a year the king paid money for his return.

When he returned to England, Chaucer worked for the king, his family and friends. In about 1367 he married Philippa de Roet, a lady who worked for the Queen.

Chaucer was a great reader and he had an excellent memory. He learned to read in Latin, French, Anglo-Norman and Italian. He knew a lot about literature, history and science.

The king often sent him to other countries on important business for him. On two of these journeys Chaucer went to Italy; first to Genoa, in 1372, and then to Milan, in 1378. People think that Chaucer became interested in Italian story-tellers on these journeys. He probably met the Italian writer, Boccaccio, when he was in Italy. We can be sure that he read Boccaccio's book, the *Decameron* (1348–58).

Chaucer became a rich man during this time, but in December 1386 he lost his job. John of Gaunt, the king's son and Chaucer's friend, left England to fight in Spain. The Duke of Gloucester took his place and he didn't like Chaucer. He gave Chaucer's job to his friends. So Chaucer had more time for writing, and he began work on *The Canterbury Tales*.

In 1389 John of Gaunt returned to England and gave Chaucer an important job again. Chaucer was growing old. He felt that his writing was getting worse. He died on 25 October, 1400, and his body was put in Westminster Abbey.

We do not know exactly when Chaucer started writing poems. It was probably when he returned from the war in France.

Chaucer wrote a lot of poems, and some of his great books are *The Book of the Duchess* (1369–70), *The House of Fame*, *The Parliament of Fowls* (between 1372 and 1382), and *Troilius and Criseyde* (between 1380 and 1385). His most famous work is *The Canterbury Tales*. Chaucer worked on this from 1386 or 1387, but he never finished the book.

Printing was introduced in Germany in about 1450. In 1477 Caxton made the first machine which could print in England. He printed *The Canterbury Tales* in 1478.

The Canterbury Tales was not the first book of short stories. Chaucer's idea – a group of people who each tell a story – wasn't a new idea either. In Boccaccio's *Decameron*, ten people escape to the country from a terrible illness in Florence. Each person tells a story to pass the time.

In *The Canterbury Tales*, the story-tellers are pilgrims. Their stories are interesting, but the pilgrims also seem very real to us. We feel we know them personally by the end of their stories. They are ordinary people – rich and poor, intelligent and stupid, young and old, from the town and from the country. They do not do the same jobs as we do today. But we all know people like them. The pilgrims' stories help us to understand English life in Chaucer's time.

The pilgrims' stories are all completely different, and they come from all over Europe. Some of the stories even come from countries in the East. At that time, people in Europe loved stories which taught them something – stories with a message about life or a new idea.

The stories in *The Canterbury Tales* are told like poems, and they are written in Chaucer's English. For this Penguin Reader we have chosen seven of the pilgrims' stories, and we have written them in modern English.

Some of the People in this Book

clerk

pardoner

knight

friar

summoner

nun

franklin

priest

The Prologue

At the Tabard Inn

Pilgrims are people who travel to special places because they want to please God. Their journeys are often to places where a saint lived or died. Thomas à Becket was a saint. He was killed in Canterbury, in a great old church. Years ago, pilgrims went to Canterbury to visit this church.

This book tells the story of some pilgrims who travelled from London to Canterbury together. On the journey each person had to tell a story – a tale.

◆

The pilgrims met at a place called the Tabard Inn in London. The fat owner of the inn was always happy. He told amusing stories which made the pilgrims laugh. They had a good meal at his inn, with a lot of excellent food and drink.

After the meal, the fat man stood up and said, 'Friends, I'm very pleased to meet you. As you know, it's a long way to Canterbury. You need to stay happy on the journey. I've got an idea. You must all tell a story on the way. We'll give a free dinner to the person who tells the best story. Now, put up your hands if you agree.'

The pilgrims all held up their hands and cried out, 'Yes! Yes! That's a good idea. And *you* can decide which story is best.'

The next morning they all got up very early and started on their journey. After a time, they stopped and gave their horses water. Then the fat man said, 'Now, who's going to tell the first story? Sir Knight, will you?'

The knight was travelling to Canterbury for a special reason. He wanted to thank God because he was safe after a dangerous war.

'Yes, all right,' he said. 'I'll begin.'

And he started to tell his story.

1

The next morning they all got up very early and
started on their journey.

The Knight's Tale

Palamon and Arcite

Many years ago in Greece, there was a great soldier called Duke Theseus. He and his wife, Queen Hippolyta, were the most important people in Athens. The queen's beautiful younger sister, Emily, lived with them.

One day, a soldier brought the duke some bad news.

'Creon has begun a war against you, Duke Theseus. And he has won Thebes already.'

When he heard this, Theseus and his knights rode to Thebes. There they fought Creon and killed him.

Two rich young knights in Thebes fought for Creon. Their names were Palamon and Arcite and they were hurt in the fighting. They were taken to see Theseus at the end of the war.

'Your families will pay a lot of gold if I free you,' the duke said to them. 'But you're my enemies. You fought against me, and you'll never be free again.'

The two knights were locked in a high tower in Athens. Then the duke rode home to Queen Hippolyta and her sister, Emily.

◆

Palamon and Arcite were prisoners in the tower for many years.

One morning, Palamon got up early and looked out of the window at the duke's garden. There he saw the queen's beautiful sister, Emily. She was walking in the garden with flowers in her hair.

When Palamon saw her, he cried out. She was so beautiful.

'Dear Palamon, what's the matter?' asked Arcite in a worried voice. 'Your face has gone white! Why did you cry out?'

'I've just seen the most beautiful lady in the world,' Palamon answered. 'Please God, get me out of this prison. If I can't make her my wife, then I want to die!'

Arcite jumped up quickly and looked out of the window. When he saw Emily he also fell in love with her.

'If she can't love me, I don't want to live,' he cried.

Palamon was very angry when he heard this. 'But you can't steal my lady like that! I fell in love with her first, and I'll love her for ever. You must help me to win her.'

'You saw her first, but I love her as much as you do!' answered Arcite angrily. 'And how can you or I win her? We're prisoners in this terrible tower.'

'Perhaps we'll be free one day, and then the best man will marry her,' said Palamon sadly. Life seemed very hard to both the young men.

◆

Duke Theseus had a good friend in Athens called Duke Perotheus. Perotheus knew the young knight, Arcite, and liked him very much. When he heard that Arcite was a prisoner in the tower, he said to Theseus, 'I'm very sorry that Arcite's your prisoner. He's not like Creon, you know. He's a good young man. Dear friend, please free him so he can live in the real world again.'

Duke Theseus thought hard and then answered, 'Perotheus, you're my good friend, so I'll free Arcite for you. But he must leave Athens, and never return. If he does return, I'll cut off his head!'

◆

Before Arcite left the tower, he talked to Palamon. 'I must leave Athens, but you can stay here and look at my beautiful lady in the garden. You're luckier than me.'

But Palamon was as sad as Arcite. 'You'll be free. Perhaps you'll return to Athens with soldiers one day and fight Theseus. And if you win, my beautiful lady will be yours.'

Then the two knights said goodbye and Arcite left the tower.

The young knight went back to Thebes, but he was very sad without his beautiful Emily. He thought about her every day and every night, and soon he became very ill.

One night, the god Mercury visited him in his sleep and said, 'Go back to Athens, Arcite. Then you'll be happy again.'

Arcite jumped out of bed and cried, 'Yes, I'll go back immediately! If the duke catches me, he'll cut off my head. But I'm not afraid of death if I can see my beautiful lady again.'

Then he looked at his face in the mirror. He looked very different because of his illness.

'Nobody will know me now,' he thought. 'I can go to Athens safely.'

So Arcite went back to Athens. Nobody knew who he was. He became one of Emily's servants – he got her water, cut wood, and worked very hard for her. He stayed in Emily's house for seven years and he was soon very popular. Even Duke Theseus began to notice him.

◆

All this time, poor Palamon was a prisoner in the tower. He was very unhappy but he couldn't escape. A man watched him all day and all night.

One day, one of Palamon's friends had an idea. He put some poison into this man's drink. The man fell asleep and Palamon took his key, opened the great door, and was free at last!

'I'll return to Thebes now,' he thought. 'But I'll come back to Athens soon with a lot of soldiers and kill Theseus. Then I'll marry Emily.'

He ran away from the tower as fast as he could. He planned to walk all night and hide during the day. When the sun came up, he rested in a wood.

That morning, Arcite was riding in the wood, singing in the sunshine. He didn't know that Palamon was hiding there.

'Emily still doesn't know me,' he said to himself sadly. 'I'm only her servant. She's got no idea who I really am. What can I do to win her love?'

Palamon was hiding behind a tree near Arcite. When he heard this, his face went as white as death. 'Arcite!' he shouted. 'I'm going to kill you! You were like a brother to me once, but you still love my lady. You or I must die!'

Arcite was very surprised to see Palamon. But he answered quietly, 'Love is free, isn't it? I'll always love Emily, but let's fight for her tomorrow. I'll meet you here. If you win, the lady will be yours.'

'Good! I'll see you here tomorrow!' answered Palamon, walking away angrily.

◆

The next morning, Palamon and Arcite met again and the great fight began. Duke Theseus, Queen Hippolyta and Emily were riding in the wood and heard the sound of fighting. Soon they saw the two knights.

'Stop!' shouted Theseus. 'Why are you fighting like this?'

'Sir, we're two unhappy men,' answered Arcite in a tired voice. 'You're our lord. Kill me first. Then kill my friend.'

'This is Arcite,' Palamon said. 'Do you remember him? He works in Princess Emily's house. But he isn't really a servant. He's worked in her house all these years because he loves her. And I am Palamon. I escaped from your tower. I love Emily too. I'm happy to die now at her feet. Kill me, but kill Arcite too.'

The duke was very angry. He wanted to kill them both.

'Yes! You must both die!' he shouted.

But the queen, Emily and all their ladies began to cry. 'No! No! These two fine young men mustn't die!'

Then the ladies all fell on their knees in front of the duke. 'Oh, sir! Please don't kill Palamon and Arcite!'

'All right,' Theseus said. 'You can live. But you must promise me that you'll never make war on my land. You must always be my friends.'

'We promise, sir,' the knights said. 'We'll always be your friends.'

'Emily can't marry both of you,' continued the duke, 'but I've got a plan. Go home to Thebes and come back in one year. Each of you must bring a hundred knights, ready to fight for you. Emily will marry the winner. Do you agree?'

Palamon and Arcite both looked at Emily on her horse. They fell on their knees and thanked Theseus again and again. Then they went home to Thebes and began to get ready for the great fight.

◆

Duke Theseus was busy too. He built a place outside Athens for the fight. It had stone walls, with white gates on the east and west sides. The duke built three temples – a temple of Venus, the goddess of love; a temple of Diana, the goddess of the moon; and a temple of Mars, the god of war.

There were beautiful pictures in the temple of Venus, and a garden full of flowers. The temple of Diana had a picture of the moon. The temple of Mars was very different. It was an unhappy place with pictures of wars and burning towns. In the middle was a picture of Mars with a fire in front of him.

◆

After a year, Palamon and Arcite returned to Athens, and each of them had his hundred knights. When they heard about the temples, they both wanted to visit them.

Palamon thought, 'I'm going to the temple of Venus. She'll help me. I'll ask her for a quick death if I lose.'

So he went to Venus's temple and the goddess seemed to move her head.

Palamon and Arcite both looked at Emily on her horse.

When Palamon saw this, he cried out, 'Oh, I'm so happy. Venus has moved her head. That means she's going to help me!'

Arcite went to the temple of Mars, the god of war.

'Mars, please help me to win,' he said in the temple.

Suddenly the temple doors began to move and the fire in front of Mars burned strongly. Then a low voice said, 'You *will* win, Arcite!'

Arcite was very happy when he heard this. 'Mars is going to help me! I'm going to win!'

◆

Now, pilgrims, you're going to hear how Mars and Venus kept their promises.

The next morning everyone in Athens went to see the great fight. There were lords and knights in fine clothes, and beautiful ladies in wonderful dresses. Duke Theseus, Queen Hippolyta and Emily sat and watched it all.

When everyone was quiet, a soldier cried out, 'Duke Theseus doesn't want anyone to die today. If you are hurt, you will become a prisoner. If Palamon or Arcite become prisoners, then the fighting will end. Now, let's begin!'

Arcite then came onto the field through the west gate, near the temple of Mars. His clothes were all red. Palamon came through the east gate, near the temple of Venus. His clothes were all white.

Pilgrims, I can't tell you everything about the great fight. Horses fell to the ground, brave men were hurt, servants brought food and drink to the fighters. Then, at the end of the day, Palamon was hurt and the fighting stopped.

'Arcite can marry Emily now,' said the duke. 'He's won her in this long day's fight!'

'Arcite's the winner!' shouted the people. 'Arcite! Arcite!'

There was loud music and Arcite rode proudly across the field towards Emily. She looked down at him and thought, 'He's so brave and handsome! I'm sure I can love him!'

But suddenly something frightened Arcite's horse. The horse fell to the ground and Arcite was thrown off. People ran to him and carried him carefully to Theseus's house. They put him on a bed and waited for the doctor.

'He's very ill,' said the doctor when he came. 'I'm afraid he's going to die.'

Arcite sent for Palamon and Emily. 'I've loved you so much, Emily,' he said sadly. 'I've been unhappy and ill because of you. And now I'm going to die for you. If you want a husband, marry Palamon. It will make me happy when I'm dead.'

Then he closed his eyes. Just before he died he looked up at Emily. He said her name.

When they heard the news, the people of Athens felt very sad. They cried for many days.

◆

Months passed. Time makes most things better. The people of Athens were tired of all the fighting and they wanted to be friends with the people of Thebes. So Duke Theseus decided to send for Palamon.

When Palamon arrived in Athens, he was wearing black clothes for his lost friend, Arcite. 'Don't be sad,' the duke said to him. 'You'll never forget your dear friend but you can still be happy. Remember what Arcite said to Emily: "If you want a husband, marry Palamon." Does that make you feel happier?'

Then the duke called for Emily and took her hand. 'Emily, all my people want to be friends with the people of Thebes. If you agree to marry Palamon, then we'll stop being enemies. Take good Palamon, Emily, and marry him. He's loved you for a long time.'

Then he turned to Palamon, 'Sir, take this lady by the hand. She'll be your dear wife.'

So Palamon and Emily were married and lived happily together. And the people of Athens and Thebes were never enemies again.

◆

At the end of the story, all the pilgrims said, 'That was a beautiful story, Knight!'

Some of the other pilgrims told their stories. Then the fat man turned to the Clerk of Oxford. 'You haven't said a word since we started our journey, Clerk. Perhaps you're thinking about your books. Well, now think about us. Have you got a good story to tell us?'

The Clerk of Oxford was very poor and his clothes were old. He and his horse never had enough food. But he loved books and he loved teaching people. He was happy to begin his story.

The Clerk's Tale

Patient Griselda

'My story is about a patient wife,' the clerk said. All the pilgrims listened carefully as he began his tale.

◆

Walter, a great lord, lived in a beautiful part of Italy, . He was young, strong and handsome, and kind to all his people.

Walter wasn't married and this made his people very sad. One day, they went to see him. They asked him to listen to them. A wise old man spoke for all of them.

'Sir, we've come to talk to you because you're a good man. We want to tell you what's in our hearts. Don't be angry with us. Please get married, then we'll be happy. Your wife will love you and look after you, and you'll have children. We'll find a wife for you if you want. She'll be beautiful and rich!'

Walter laughed at the old man's words, but he was pleased.

'You know, my dear people, I like being free,' he answered. 'I don't want a wife, but perhaps I need one. So, yes, I *will* get married very soon. But *I'll* choose my wife! And when I marry her, I want you all to talk to her like a princess. You must do this for me.'

Walter's people were very happy. 'Yes, of course we'll do that, sir,' they all said. And they went back to their homes and waited for the wedding day.

◆

A very poor man lived near Walter's house. His name was Janicula. He had a beautiful daughter called Griselda. She was a kind girl and she looked after her old father well. She worked hard in their little house, and in the fields with their animals. She worked outside in the wind and the rain. Walter often saw her when he was riding in the country.

'She's the most beautiful girl I've ever seen,' he thought to himself. 'I'd like to marry *her*.' But he didn't tell anyone about Griselda and his love for her.

The day of the wedding arrived. Walter's great house was full of people. Everything was ready for the big day.

'Follow me,' Walter said to all the lords and ladies.

He went out to the fields where some of his people lived. The lords and ladies followed him. 'What's he going to do?' they asked in surprise.

◆

That morning, Griselda finished her work early because she wanted to see Walter's new wife. She thought, 'I'll stand with the other girls and watch Sir Walter with his beautiful lady. But first I must help my dear father to sit in the sun.'

She opened the door of the little house from inside – and there was Walter! He was standing outside in his rich clothes, like a king.

'Griselda,' he said, 'where's your father?'

The old man came slowly out of the house and Walter took his hand.

'Janicula, I must tell you what's in my heart. I love your daughter, Griselda. I want to marry her if you'll agree.'

The old man was too surprised to speak at first. After some minutes he answered, 'Yes, sir, of course. If Griselda agrees, she can be your wife.'

'I'd like to speak to her in your house, please,' Walter said quietly. 'I'll ask her to be my wife. But she must promise me something. She must always do what I ask.'

The people outside waited. They couldn't understand what was happening!

Inside the house, Walter spoke softly to Griselda.

'My dear Griselda, your father says that we can get married. Please take me as your husband. But first I must ask you this. Will you promise to do what I tell you – always?'

'My lord,' Griselda answered, 'I'll marry you if I can look after my father in my new life. And I'll always do everything you tell me to do.'

'Thank you, my dear Griselda,' said Walter.

He asked some of the ladies to come inside and dress Griselda in beautiful clothes. Then he kissed her hand and took her outside.

'This is my new wife, everybody,' he said proudly.

When Griselda came out of the house, the people cried out, 'She's the most beautiful girl we've ever seen!'

Walter was very happy. They were married that day and there was music and dancing all night.

◆

For a long time all Walter's people lived happily. Griselda helped poor and sick people and everyone loved her. People said, 'Our great lord did a wise thing when he married Griselda.'

Then Walter and Griselda had a little girl and everyone said, 'One day this little girl will be as kind and as beautiful as her mother.'

But from that time things started to go very wrong.

Every day Walter watched his wife with her baby and thought, 'My wife will change now because she's got a child. If I ask her to do something difficult for me, she won't do it.'

Then Walter did something very bad. He came to see Griselda one day with a hard look on his face.

'Griselda, when I married you, my people were unhappy,' he lied. 'You were a poor man's daughter. Now you've got a child, and it's even worse for them. I'm going to ask someone to take this child away from you. You must give her to him. Remember your words on your wedding day!'

Griselda was very sad, but she said, 'My child is yours, my lord. You can do what you want with her.'

Walter was happy when he heard this. He quickly sent a man to take the child away. When Griselda saw the man, she said quietly, 'I must kiss my daughter before she goes.'

Then she took her child in her arms and said, 'Goodbye, my dear daughter. I'll never see you again but God will look after you.'

Then the man took Griselda's daughter away.

'Please put her little body in the ground,' she called out to him. 'Then it will be safe from all the animals and birds.'

The man carried the child to Walter. 'Take her to my sister in Bologna,' he said. 'Tell her to look after her well. But don't tell her that she's my child.'

◆

Walter watched Griselda closely after this. She seemed to love him in the same way, but she was very quiet and her face often looked sad.

After some months a little boy was born. Walter's people were very happy. 'One day this child will be our prince. One day we shall be his people,' they said.

But after two years Walter had another plan. He wanted to be sure that his wife loved him. So he decided to test her again.

He went to Griselda and said, 'Griselda, my people don't want Janicula's grandson to be their prince. Once again, you must give your child to my man.'

'My lord,' she answered, 'I'll always do everything that you want. Take our son. And if you'll be happier without me too, please tell me. I'll die if it will please you. I only want to keep your love.'

Nothing could change the feelings in Walter's heart. He

Then the man took Griselda's daughter away.

sent the same man to take away her little boy. Again, she kissed her child before he left her for ever. And again she said to the man, 'Put his little body in the ground. Then no animal or bird can hurt him.' Walter sent the little boy to Bologna to live with his sister.

Walter watched his wife carefully again. He saw that her patience and love for him never changed. But his people were angry with him. They talked about him all over the country.

'He's killed his two children!' they said. 'He didn't want Lady Griselda to love them. She must only love *him*! And she never changes. She still loves him and looks after all of us.'

◆

One day, Walter had another idea. He decided to send Griselda away and get a new wife. When Griselda heard about this, she thought, 'This is the worst thing that's ever happened to me. I love my husband more than anything in the world. How can I ever live without him?' She felt very sad.

First, Walter wrote a letter to his sister in Bologna. It said:

Please bring the two children to me. Tell everyone, 'This little girl's going to be Walter's new wife.' But don't tell anyone who sent the children to you years ago.

When she received this letter, his sister left Bologna with the two children. The little boy and girl were very beautiful. They were dressed in rich clothes and rode on fine horses.

Walter then called for Griselda and, in a room full of people, said to her, 'Griselda, you've been a good wife to me. But now I must change my way of life. My people want me to send you away and marry a new wife – a girl from a rich family. She's on her way here now.'

Griselda's answer moved the hearts of all the people who

heard her. But it didn't move the hard heart of her husband.

'I'm not good enough for you, my lord,' she said sadly. 'I've always known that. Thank you for the beautiful home that I've lived in for so long. I'll gladly go back to my father now if you and your people want me to do that. I'll always love you and I'll never marry again. I thought you loved me too. But the old words are very true: "As men grow old, love grows cold." I must leave everything behind me here. I'll just take my old clothes.'

Then she put on her poorest clothes and began the long walk home. Many people followed her with tears in their eyes. They were very sad that Griselda was leaving like this. When her father saw her, he ran out of his house. He took his poor daughter in his arms.

◆

For a time Griselda lived quietly with her father. It was like the old days. She worked in the little house and looked after the animals in the fields. But one day Walter sent for her.

'Griselda,' he said, 'I want to make my new wife as happy as possible. You must help me. You know my house and you looked after me well. You must leave your home and work for my new wife. Start now and make everything ready for her.'

'My lord, I'll be happy to help you and your new wife,' Griselda answered. And she began work immediately. She cleaned all the gold and silver, made the beds and washed the floors. She told the servants in the house to work hard. She worked harder than everyone.

Later that day, many people came to Walter's house to see his new wife. Griselda met them and led them to their places. Then Walter brought in a beautiful young girl. He turned to Griselda and asked her, 'Do you like my new young wife?'

'I've never seen anyone who is more beautiful,' she answered. 'I hope you'll be very happy together. I only ask one thing – be kind to her. I was poor when I came here. But she's a lady and it will be harder for her. She'll be very unhappy if you're unkind to her.'

Walter finally realized that Griselda really loved him. He said to himself, 'I've been very bad. I've hurt Griselda but she still loves me.'

He turned to her and cried, 'Griselda! Griselda! Please forgive me! I'll never hurt you again or make you sad. Now I know that you'll always be true to me.' And he took her in his arms and kissed her again and again.

Walter told Griselda everything and then he brought the children to her. 'This is your daughter, my dear. I'm not really going to marry her. And this is our son. I sent them both to Bologna, to live with my sister. She looked after them well, and they've been safe and happy all these years.'

When Griselda saw her children, she cried with happiness. She put her arms round them and kissed them.

'Oh, thank you, my lord!' she said to Walter, with tears in her eyes. 'I can die happily now. I have both my children *and* your love!'

Then her ladies took her to her rooms, took off her old clothes, and dressed her in her beautiful rich clothes. She was Walter's wife again.

◆

Walter and Griselda lived happily together for many years. Janicula, Griselda's old father, came to live with them. Their daughter married a rich, handsome man. And when Walter died, their son became a lord and was loved by all his people.

◆

'Well, that's the end of my story,' said the clerk. 'But in my opinion, Griselda was *too* patient. Husbands, don't test the patience of your wives like Walter did. I'm sure they won't all be as patient as poor Griselda!

'And I want to say something to the wives too. Don't be afraid of your husband. Your words will always win a fight, even against a big, strong man!'

The Wife of Bath's Tale

What do women want most?

Most of the pilgrims on their way to Canterbury were men. There were only a few women. One of them was the Wife of Bath. She was a large woman with a red face. She wore a big hat, and she rode on a very fat horse. She was rich and all her five husbands were dead!

The Wife of Bath was a happy woman and she loved to talk. This is her story about a knight at the time of King Arthur and his Knights of the Round Table.

◆

Long ago, there was a young knight who did a very bad thing. He broke the law that all the knights had to live by. When King Arthur heard this, he was very angry.

'This knight must die!' he shouted.

But the queen and her ladies were sad because they liked the young knight very much.

'Please, please,' they cried to King Arthur, 'don't end this young man's life. He'll never make the same mistake again.'

The king turned to the queen and said, 'All right, do what you like with him, my dear. But we must punish him because he's broken the law.'

The queen thought for a short time, and then she said to the knight, 'You can live if you tell me the answer to this question: What does a woman want most in all the world? I'll give you a year and a day to find the answer. If you can't find the answer, then you'll die.'

The knight thanked the queen, but he rode away very sadly.

'The queen has asked me a very difficult question. How can I find the answer?' he thought to himself.

◆

As he rode through the country, the knight asked a lot of people the queen's question. He was given many different answers.

One man said, 'Ah, that's easy. Women like money more than anything.'

A woman answered, 'What do women want most in all the world? They want to be happy, of course.'

Another woman replied, 'Fine clothes. That's what they want.'

Then the knight asked some children the same question.

A little girl said, 'My mother's happy when she's cooking good food for us.'

And a little boy replied, 'My mother likes having a new baby in the family.'

'Our mother's happy when she sees our father come home at night,' said two or three children.

Many of the answers seemed good, but they were all different. 'Nobody agrees,' thought the knight sadly. 'How can I find the right answer to the queen's question?'

◆

After a year, the knight had to return to the queen and give her the answer to her question.

'What can I say?' he thought. 'I've tried so hard to find the right answer! But I know I'm going to die.'

But then he came to a great wood. In the trees he saw twenty-four beautiful ladies! They were all laughing and singing and dancing on the green grass.

'I've got enough time to ask these ladies the question,' he said to himself.

He turned his horse towards the ladies ... but where were

they? He could only see one very ugly, old woman! When he came near her, she stood up. She smiled at him.

'Sir Knight, are you looking for something?' she asked. 'Tell me what it is. Perhaps I can help you. We old people are wise and we know many things.'

'You're right – perhaps you *can* help me,' answered the knight. 'I have to find the answer to a question or I'll die. The question is: What does a woman want most in all the world? If you can tell me, I'll give you a lot of money.'

'Give me your hand, sir,' replied the old woman. 'I'll tell you the right answer if you promise me something. You have to do the first thing that I ask you.'

That sounded easy to the knight. 'I promise,' he answered in an excited voice. Perhaps the old woman could *really* help him!

'Good, then your life's safe,' said the old woman. 'Nobody – not even the queen – will say that your answer is wrong.'

Then she spoke very quietly into the knight's ear. 'That's the answer to your question,' she said with a smile.

The knight smiled back at the old woman and thanked her with all his heart. Then they went together to meet the queen and all the lords and ladies.

◆

Everyone heard that the young knight was coming. They were very excited, but a lot of people were worried about his answer.

'It was a very difficult question,' they said. 'It will be terrible if he can't give the queen the right answer. He will die!'

The queen and her lords and ladies met the knight. The queen started to speak and everyone listened carefully.

'Now, Sir Knight, can you answer my question? What does a woman want most in all the world?' she asked in a clear voice.

The knight came up to the queen and fell on his knees in front of her. All the people around them heard his words.

'My lady, I know the right answer to your question. All women want to be the head of their house. They want their husbands to do what they say!'

When they heard this, everyone laughed and shouted, 'He must live! He must live! That's the right answer!'

The queen smiled at the knight. She was very pleased with his answer.

'You will be free, Sir Knight,' she said. 'You can live!'

But suddenly the ugly old woman walked towards the queen and said, 'Be good to me too, my lady. I said to this knight, "I'll tell you the right answer. But you must promise me something. You have to do the first thing that I ask you." And you agreed, didn't you?' she said, turning to the knight.

'Yes, madam,' said the young knight. 'That's what I promised.'

'Well, I want you to marry me!' said the old woman. Her face looked very ugly when she said these terrible words.

The knight replied unhappily, 'I made a promise to you, it's true. But I can't marry you!'

'I'm old, ugly and poor but I want to be your wife,' cried the old woman. 'I want to win your love.'

'My love!' laughed the knight. 'You can't really hope for that!'

The queen and all the people around her were laughing.

'The knight wants to die now!' they shouted. 'He doesn't want to marry this ugly old woman!'

But the queen looked at the knight and said, 'You must marry her, Sir Knight. You promised.'

'Yes, I know,' answered the knight unhappily. 'I can't break my promise.'

◆

There was no dancing or singing at the wedding. There were no fine clothes or good food. At the end of the day, the knight sadly carried away his new wife.

At the end of the day, the knight sadly carried away his new wife.

That night, the ugly old woman turned to the knight and said, 'Come here, my dear husband. Why are you looking so unhappy? What have I done wrong? Tell me, and I'll try to do better. I'll make you happy.'

'Do better? You can't become a young woman and you can't make yourself beautiful!' answered the knight.

'Is that the only problem?' she asked with a smile on her face.

'That's enough!' he answered.

'I'm not beautiful,' said the old woman, 'but that's only on the outside. Faces become old but hearts are always young. A person with a good heart is better than someone who does bad things.'

Then the woman talked quietly to her husband for a long time. He was very surprised when he heard her words.

'You're very wise and good,' he said at last. 'You've taught me a lot about men and women, and about good and bad.'

'Is it better to have a beautiful wife who makes you unhappy?' she asked. 'Or an old and ugly wife who is kind to you?'

'My lady, my love, and my dear wife,' said the knight softly, 'you're right. I'll always do what you tell me.'

She laughed. 'Remember the answer to the question! Can I be the head of our home?'

'Yes, my love, of course you can,' said the knight.

Then she kissed him and said, 'Don't be angry. I'll be a good wife to you. And I'll be as beautiful as a queen!'

The knight started to kiss his wife, but he suddenly jumped back in surprise! There, in front of him, stood the most beautiful girl in the world! His wife wasn't really an ugly old woman. She was a fairy!

'I wanted to be sure that you are a true knight,' she said. 'Now I know that you're a good person. Now I don't have to be an ugly old woman!'

The knight kissed his beautiful young wife and then they went to see the queen. Everybody was very surprised when they saw the young woman. They all danced and sang when they heard the story.

The knight and his wife lived happily together all their lives. And they always remembered the answer to the queen's question.

◆

'That's the end of my story,' said the Wife of Bath to the other pilgrims. 'Please God, send us husbands who are young and loving! Men, do what your wives tell you to do! And give them a lot of money to spend!'

The Pardoner's Tale

Three Men Look for Death

The pardoner told his story next. But first, he told the other pilgrims about his job.

'I speak to people in churches,' he said. 'I always talk about the same thing. I tell people: "Love of money is a real problem. You do bad things, and bad things happen to you, because of it." And I sell pardons. I've got a lot of things that belonged to saints – bits of cloth and other old things. Well, they didn't really belong to saints, but people don't know that! If people buy these things, God will forgive them. And I make a lot of money. I don't like being poor. Oh no! I must have fine clothes and good food! The poor give me money and I have a good life. I sell them pardons and they're happy.'

The pardoner was a very bad man but his story was very good. The pilgrims were surprised that a bad man could tell a good tale.

This is the story.

◆

There were three young men who did many bad and stupid things. They drank too much and they did no work.

One morning, they were drinking when they heard a noise outside. People were carrying the body of a dead man.

They asked the boy who brought them more drink, 'Whose body is that, boy?'

'He was your friend,' answered the boy. 'He was killed last night while he was drinking here. He was killed by that quiet thief, Death. Death kills all the people in this country. He killed your friend and then went away. He's killed thousands and thousands of people. You should get ready to meet Death.'

'I'm not afraid to meet him!' cried one young man, and he quickly jumped up. 'I'm going to find him! I'll look for him in every field and wood and town. Listen! Let's hold up our hands and promise to be brothers. Let's find Death and kill him!'

'I'll come with you,' said the second man.

'And me,' said the third. 'We'll kill this dangerous man, Death, before night comes.'

So the three men went to find Death. They walked a little way and saw an old man with a long white beard. He was wearing a lot of old clothes and carrying a stick. When he saw the three men, he spoke to them kindly.

'God be with you, my young friends.'

But the men shouted at him, 'You stupid old man! Why are you wearing all those clothes?'

'Because I'm very old,' answered the man. 'I feel the cold and I can never get warm.'

'Well, why have you lived for so long then, you ugly old man? You should die more quickly!' they shouted.

The old man looked at them angrily. 'I live like this because Death hasn't taken me. I travel up and down the country, looking for Death. I say to the ground under my feet: "Dear Mother Earth, let me in! Oh, Mother Earth, I want to lie down in you and sleep for ever!" But she isn't kind to me. That's why I'm old, young men.'

One of the men laughed loudly. The old man turned to him and said quietly, 'You've spoken very unkindly to me and now you're laughing at me. But I've done nothing to hurt you. You should speak more kindly to an old man. Now, I've got nothing more to say to you. I'm going to continue on my journey to meet Death.'

'No, you can't do that!' they shouted. 'He's killed all our

They walked a little way and saw an old man with a long white beard.

friends in this country. We're going to find him and kill *him*. Quickly, tell us where he is.'

'If you really want to find Death, I'll tell you,' answered the old man. 'Can you see that little road? Go up there. Not long ago I saw him near a great tree in the wood. But you can't save men from Death. He won't be afraid of you. Go now. I hope God will help you to become better men.'

◆

The three young men went up the road and ran towards the great tree, but there was nobody there. They sat down and looked around them. Then suddenly, on the ground, they saw a lot of money. They all got very excited and forgot about Death. But Death was very near and he was thinking about them.

Nobody said anything as they started to count the money. At last one of them spoke.

'Listen to me,' he said. 'This money will bring us happiness for the rest of our lives but we must hide it. One of us must go back to the town for food and drink. The other two can hide in the wood. They must guard the money until night comes.'

This plan sounded sensible. So the youngest man went into town and his two friends waited in the wood with the money.

'I've got an idea,' said one of the men. 'We're like three brothers, but one of us has gone now. If you take half the money, I'll take the other half. Then we'll be really rich!'

'But how can we do that?' asked the other man. 'Our young brother knows about the money.'

'I'll tell you how we can do it. There are two of us. Two men are stronger than one. When he comes back, we'll play a game with him. You can start a friendly fight with him. I'll wait and then kill him with my knife. After that, my dear brother, we can take all the money. Half for you and half for me!'

And so they planned their young friend's death.

But the young friend was bad too. As he walked to the town, his mind was full of the beautiful money. He said to himself, 'How can I get all that money? If I think of a good plan, I'll be the happiest, richest man in the world!'

At last he had an idea.

'I know what I'll do. I'll go to a shop and buy some poison. Then I'll kill the other two and take all the money.'

So he went to a shop in the town and said to the shopkeeper, 'The cats on my farm are eating all my plants. Can you give me something to kill them?'

The shopkeeper showed him a small bottle of poison.

'This will kill your cats,' he said. 'Put it in their food or drinking water. It's very strong. It will kill a horse!'

Then the young man went to the next street and bought three bottles of wine. He put the poison into two of the bottles and he kept the third bottle.

'I'll need a drink after I've killed my two friends. I'll hide their bodies first and then hide the money. I'll need a good bottle of wine after all that!'

Then he bought some food and walked back to the wood. When the other two men saw him, they said, 'Ha! Here he comes! He's bringing us our supper but *he'll* never have another meal again!'

They were hungry and they ate the food immediately. Then the two men asked their young friend to play the fighting game. Their plan went well and they soon killed him.

'Let's eat again and drink some of this wine. Then we'll put his body in the ground,' they said.

One man got a bottle of wine and drank a lot of it. Then he gave the bottle to the other man.

Both men died slowly in a lot of pain.

They wanted to find Death and kill him. But when Death found them, they were all dead!

And Death laughed loudly for a long time!

◆

'Well, that's the end of my story,' said the pardoner. 'Now, I've got some things here in my bag. They'll bring you forgiveness and save you all. Only a penny! Hurry! Hurry! Come and buy!'

The Franklin's Tale

Three Promises

The franklin was a rich farmer. He had a big house and a lot of land, and he liked good food and wine. His guests always had excellent things to eat and drink when they came to visit him.

The franklin told the pilgrims a story about three promises.

◆

Long ago, in France, there lived a knight called Arveragus. He was in love with a beautiful lady called Dorigen. She wanted to be sure that he was brave and good. So she asked him to do a lot of difficult things.

'Do these things for me. Then I'll know that you love me,' she said to him.

Arveragus went away and had many adventures. He did all the things that Dorigen asked him to do. Then he came back to his love, Dorigen.

'Now I know that you aren't afraid of anything,' Dorigen said to him. 'I love you as much as you love me. I want to marry you.'

The knight loved his lady very much. 'I want to marry you, too,' he said. 'I'll never ask you to do anything that you don't want to do,' he told her.

'And when we're married,' she said, 'I'll be your loving wife. I'll never do anything that will make you unhappy.'

◆

Arveragus and Dorigen got married and went to live in Arveragus's home in Brittany. They lived together happily for more than a year. But the knight was a man of war and he wanted to fight in England. Even his love for his wife couldn't stop him.

So he sailed away for two years.

◆

Poor Dorigen was left at home. She felt very sad without her husband, because she loved him very much. She couldn't sleep or eat when he was away.

Her friends tried hard to help her.

'You'll die if you don't sleep and eat more,' they said to her.

She listened to her friends and slowly got better. She was young and full of hope.

'My husband's going to come home soon,' she thought.

Arveragus sent her long, loving letters. 'All is well,' he wrote. 'I'll be home again very soon, my love.'

Her friends said to her, 'Now you're feeling better, so come outside with us. Don't sit alone in your house. Come and have fun.'

So she began to go out with them. One day, as she was walking with her friends, Dorigen saw great black rocks in the sea. She felt very frightened when she saw them. Sometimes, when she was far away from the sea, she thought about those terrible rocks.

'I don't like those rocks. If a ship hits them, the men on the ship will die. Will my dear Arveragus be safe? Oh, why did God make something which can kill men? He loves everyone!'

Her friends saw that she was becoming ill again. They were worried. They were kind people and they wanted to help her. So they kept her away from the black rocks, and they took her out with them to other places. They danced and played games together.

◆

One day in spring, they went to a beautiful garden. They sat down on the grass and sang and danced. Only Dorigen was unhappy. All the men were dancing happily, but her dear husband, Arveragus, was not there.

One of the dancers in the garden was a man called Aurelius. He was a handsome young man and he loved Dorigen with all his heart. But he never spoke to her about his feelings. Some of his friends knew that he was in love. But they didn't know who the lady was.

When Aurelius saw Dorigen in the garden on that spring day, he couldn't hide his love.

'I know that your heart lies over the sea with Arveragus,' he said to her. 'You're his wife. I know that you can't love me. But I love you very much.'

'You must never speak to me like that again, Aurelius,' Dorigen answered. 'Arveragus is my husband and I love him with all my heart. I'll never leave him.'

Then she laughed and said, 'Aurelius, I *will* love you if you take away all the rocks from the sea. Then Arveragus can come home safely in his ship.'

'Is there no other way?' he asked.

'No, there's no other way,' said Dorigen.

◆

Aurelius went away sadly. First he spoke to the Sun God.

'Oh, Lord of the Sun, speak to your sister. Ask her to cover the rocks with the sea. Then my lady will love me. She won't break her promise, I'm sure.'

But nothing happened. The sea stayed the same and Aurelius could still see the black rocks. He got very ill and his brother looked after him. Aurelius told his brother everything.

'I must take those rocks away,' he said. 'If I can do that, then Dorigen will love me. I'll be a happy man.'

Aurelius's brother loved him and wanted to help him. He started to read books. He had to find a way to move the rocks.

ITEMS ISSUED/RENEWED
OR Mr Fardin Rahman
02/03/19 13:52:17
Idea Store Bow (IH)

nterbury tales/Strange, Joanna
01277031   DUE 23/03/19
Item(s) issued

LRS TSUNDANGBWD
DR Mr Faridal Rahman
02-03-19 15:52:11
Idea Store Bow (B)

...bury Lake Stanes, ...
...01YV031   DUE 23/03/19
Item(s) Issued

When Aurelius saw Dorigen in the garden on that spring day,
he couldn't hide his love.

After two years, Arveragus came home from the war. Dorigen and all their friends were very happy. But Aurelius didn't know that he was back. He lay at home in bed, very ill. His brother stayed close to him. He read his books and thought about the rocks all the time.

'How can I help my dear brother?' he asked himself every day.

At last he remembered something. He sat down near Aurelius's bed and spoke to him quietly.

'One day in Orleans, I saw a book in a friend's house. It was a book about magic. Perhaps that book will help us with the rocks. If we can hide the rocks for a short time, Dorigen will love you.'

Aurelius listened to his brother and felt much better. He jumped out of his bed and in a day or two they went to Orleans together.

◆

As they came near Orleans, they met a young man. He was a magician.

He said to them, 'I know why you've come here.'

And to their great surprise he told them everything about Dorigen and the rocks.

That night, they went with the young man to his house. Before they ate, he showed them many strange things. They were all done by magic. Forests came in front of their eyes, full of animals. Next they saw a river in the room. Then they saw many knights, and they even saw Aurelius with his love, Dorigen. Aurelius was dancing with her.

Before they went to bed, Aurelius decided. He said to the young man, 'If you hide those rocks, I'll pay you a thousand pounds.'

The young man agreed, and the next morning they all rode to

Brittany. It was December and the weather was very cold. When they arrived, the young man started his magic immediately. The sea began to cover the rocks. At the end of the day, Aurelius and his brother couldn't see one single rock!

◆

Aurelius was very excited. He found Dorigen and said to her, 'I still love you very much, dear lady. I know that you're married to Arveragus. But remember the promise that you made in the garden on that spring day. I've done what you told me to do. All the black rocks have disappeared!'

Then he went away and left her. Dorigen ran down to the sea and looked for the rocks.

'It's true!' she cried. 'All the rocks have gone – or the sea has hidden them. Aurelius has done what I asked. But what shall I do now?'

Arveragus was away from home for a few days, so she couldn't tell him about her problem. She lay on her bed and cried.

'What can I do? Shall I kill myself? Some women kill themselves because their husbands don't love them. But Arveragus loves me. Other women kill themselves because they love another man. I don't love Aurelius but I've made a promise. I must keep my promise. But I can't! Oh, what shall I do?'

She lay on her bed all day and night, and cried and cried.

◆

After two days, Arveragus came home. He saw that his wife was unhappy. He asked her, 'My love, why are you crying? What's the matter?'

Dorigen told him the story.

'Is that all?' he said, and looked at her lovingly. 'Is there nothing more?'

'That's enough!' she cried. 'Oh, Arveragus, what shall I do?'

'A promise is a promise, my dear. You must keep your promise – that's very important. I won't love you if you break your promise.'

'Then I must go to the garden where Aurelius told me about his love. I must wait for him there,' answered Dorigen sadly.

She kissed her husband goodbye and walked slowly towards the garden.

◆

Aurelius met Dorigen in the street. He looked very happy but Dorigen's eyes were red with tears.

'Where are you going?' he asked her.

'I've spoken to my husband. He told me to keep my promise to you. So I'm going to the garden where I first met you,' she replied unhappily.

Aurelius looked at Dorigen. He saw her sad face and felt sorry for her.

'I'm doing a very bad thing,' he thought. 'She loves her husband, Arveragus, very much.'

'Tell your husband that he's a good man,' he said to Dorigen. 'I don't want to come between a man and his wife. You're the most loving wife I've ever met.'

When she heard these kind words, Dorigen fell on her knees. She thanked him. Then, with a heart full of happiness, she ran home to her husband.

For the rest of their long life together, Arveragus looked after her like a queen and she was always his true and loving wife.

◆

But poor Aurelius didn't feel very happy. He was a worried man.

'How can I ever pay the magician all that money?' he thought. 'I'll have to sell everything that I own. And, even then, I won't have enough. Perhaps I can pay him a little every year.'

He had five hundred pounds, and he went to see the magician with this money.

'Here's all my money,' he said. 'I'll pay you the rest but, please, give me two or three years.'

'But *I* did what I promised to do. And *you* promised to pay me a thousand pounds,' shouted the magician angrily.

'Yes, I know. You kept your promise but I can't pay you,' Aurelius answered unhappily.

'Well, have you seen your lady? Does she love you now?' asked the magician when he saw Aurelius's sad face.

'No, she doesn't,' said Aurelius. 'Her husband loves her very much but he told her to keep her promise. He sent her to me but I sent her back to him. She loves her husband and she looked so unhappy. I didn't want to hurt her.'

The magician was pleased to hear this. He said, 'My dear brother, you've done the right thing. And now I'll do the right thing too. I won't take your money.'

And he said goodbye, got on his horse, and rode away.

◆

The franklin finished his story and then asked the pilgrims a question.

'My friends, now you must tell me something. Which of those three men seemed the best to you? Aurelius? Arveragus? Or the magician?'

The Friar's Tale

The Summoner and the Devil

There was a summoner and a friar on the pilgrimage to Canterbury.

Summoners found people who did bad things. They took them to an important person in the church. People often paid summoners a lot of money to forget those bad things. A friar's job was different. He asked people for money for the church.

The summoner and friar on the pilgrimage were not friends.

The friar said to the pilgrims, 'I'm going to tell you a story about summoners.'

Then the summoner said, 'And I'm going to tell you a story about friars.'

'Well, I'm going to tell my story first,' said the friar.

So the friar began.

◆

There was an important man in the church who was very bad. He only wanted people's money. A summoner worked for this man. He watched people quietly. Then he caught them when they did bad things. 'You must leave the church,' he told them. 'But if you give me a lot of money, you can come into the church again.'

◆

One day, the summoner was on his way to see an old woman. He thought that she was a bad woman. He wanted her to give him money.

On the way he met a man. The man was wearing bright red clothes and riding a brown horse.

42

The man was wearing bright red clothes and riding a brown horse.

'Where are you riding to?' asked the man.

Nobody liked the summoner, so he lied.

'I'm just going to get some money from an old woman. She has to pay the money to my lord.'

'Oh, so you're a bailiff,' said the man.

A bailiff is a man who looks after land for rich lords. He takes money from the farmers who use the land.

'Yes, that's right,' answered the summoner. 'I'm a bailiff.'

'I've got a farm which I look after for a lord,' said the man.

'Oh, that's interesting,' said the summoner. 'Tell me, how do you get your money from people?'

'I get it in many different ways,' said the man. 'I like having a lot of money, but my lord doesn't pay me much.'

'I've got my ways too,' said the summoner. 'I don't mind if people are frightened of me or unhappy. I think we're the same, you and I. What's your name?'

The man's answer gave the summoner a surprise.

'I'll tell you who I am. I'm a devil, and I live in hell!' he said.

'Oh, I thought you were an ordinary man like me,' said the summoner. 'You look like a man.'

'Devils can look like anything they want to,' laughed the devil. 'There are good reasons for this. Now, let's continue our journey.'

◆

So the man and the devil rode along the road. After a short time, they saw a man with some horses. He was hitting the horses and shouting at them.

'The devil can take you, you lazy animals!' he cried.

'Did you hear that?' the summoner asked the devil. 'Go and take his horses. He says that the devil can take them!'

'You can't believe everything you hear,' answered the devil. 'Wait. Let's see what happens.'

After a few minutes the tired horses started to walk a little faster. 'Good horses!' shouted their owner. 'Good Brock! Good old Scottie! God will save you all!'

'What did I tell you?' said the devil. 'He said one thing but he meant another thing. There's nothing for me here. Let's continue.'

◆

When the town was far behind them, the summoner said to the devil, 'You didn't do very well with the man and his horses, did you? Now I'm going to get some money from this poor old woman. Watch carefully! You can see how I do it.'

He went to the old woman's door. 'Come out!' he shouted. 'I'm sure you're doing something bad in there!'

'Who's that?' cried the old woman, coming quickly out of her house.

When she saw the summoner, she looked very frightened. 'Oh, it's you, sir,' she said.

'People are saying some very bad things about you,' said the summoner in a serious voice. 'If they're true, you'll have to go to the church. You'll have to pay them a lot of money.'

When she heard this, the old woman began to cry.

'Oh, sir, please be kind to me,' she said. 'I'm ill and I can't get to church. Can I pay *you* the money?'

'Yes, but you must pay me now,' answered the summoner. 'It will cost you twelve pennies. Quickly!'

'Twelve pennies!' cried the old woman. 'Oh, God help me! I haven't got twelve pennies! What can I do?'

'Give me your money!' shouted the summoner angrily.

'But I haven't done anything bad,' said the poor woman.

'Give me your money or I'll take your cooking pot. You were with a man who isn't your husband. You know you were!'

'No, I always loved my husband,' cried the old woman. 'I hope the blackest devil in hell carries you away! And the cooking pot too!'

45

Then the devil spoke to the old woman. 'Do you really mean what you're saying, madam?'

'Yes I do!' she answered. 'The devil can carry him away – clothes, cooking pot, everything.'

The summoner was still shouting at her. He was very angry.

'What? Will I get no money from this stupid old woman?'

'Why are you so angry?' asked the devil. 'You and the cooking pot are mine now. She gave you to me. Tonight you'll be in hell with me. You can learn about devils there and about how we do our work!'

Suddenly the devil jumped on the summoner and caught him. Then he carried him down to hell. There's a place for summoners in hell, and it's always very full!

◆

The friar finished his story and looked at all the pilgrims.

'Think hard about my story,' he said. 'We must hope that God will keep us from the devil!'

Then the summoner told his story about the friar. But it wasn't a very interesting story so I haven't put it in this book.

The Nun's Priest's Tale

Chaunticleer and the Fox

There was a nun on the pilgrimage called Madam Eglantine. A priest was travelling with her to help her on the journey. His name was John.

The knight said, 'We've had enough sad stories. Let's have a happy story now! You, priest – can you tell us a happy story?'

The nun's priest, John, thought for a minute and then answered, 'I'll try.'

So he told the story of Chaunticleer and Pertelote. Chaunticleer was a cock, and Pertelote was a hen.

This is the story.

◆

A long time ago, there was a poor old woman who lived in a small house in the country. Near her house was a wood.

The old woman was very poor, so she couldn't buy any food. She only ate the things that she grew in her garden, and the eggs from her hens.

The hens lived in the garden during the day. Chaunticleer, the cock, was the lord of the hens. The name Chaunticleer means 'sing beautifully' and he had a wonderful voice. Every morning he sang when the sun came up. During the day he sang every hour. So the old woman didn't need a clock – she could always tell the time by the cock.

Chaunticleer was the lord of seven hens. His wife was called Pertelote. She was very wise and she knew her husband very well. He told her everything and they often sang love songs together.

Chaunticleer, the cock, was the lord of the hens.

At night, Chaunticleer and the hens slept on the roof of the old woman's house.

One morning, just before the sun came up, Chaunticleer was sitting on the roof with Pertelote and the other hens. He was making a terrible noise, like someone who is very frightened. When Pertelote heard him, she felt frightened too.

'Oh, dear heart! she cried. 'What's the matter? Did you sleep badly?'

'Don't be angry with me, my love,' answered her husband. 'I've had a very bad dream and I still feel frightened. I thought I was in great danger. Please God, bring me something good and not danger.'

'What was your dream about, dearest?' asked Pertelote in a worried voice.'Tell me about it.'

'I dreamed that I was walking in our garden. Suddenly I saw an animal that looked like a dog. It wanted to kill me! It looked terrible – it was yellow and red with black ears. And it had two burning eyes that were looking straight at me! I've never felt so afraid in all my life. That's why I was crying out in my sleep.'

'Oh, I thought I had a brave husband!' cried Pertelote. 'But you're not the kind of husband that a woman wants. How can a brave man be afraid of dreams? You're having bad dreams because you eat too much!'

Pertelote knew a lot about health. She was as good as a doctor.

'You're ill, you know. That's why you dreamed about danger. When we fly down to the ground this morning, I'll show you some plants. You must eat them to get better.'

Chaunticleer was angry with his wife.

'She can't tell me what to do!' he thought. 'I haven't eaten too much. And I'm not ill. Dreams mean something.'

He said to his wife, 'Thank you for your lesson, but there are many wise books about dreams. These books say that all dreams mean something. And I know many true stories about dreams.'

49

Chaunticleer was a great talker and he read a lot of books. He started to tell his wife about three dreams which came true.

This is the first dream.

◆

One day, two pilgrims came to a town where there were a lot of people. It was very crowded, so there weren't many places to stay. In the end they had to sleep in different places. One man slept in a comfortable house, and the other man slept in a farmhouse.

In the night, the man in the comfortable house dreamed that his friend was calling him. His friend was crying, 'Help! Help! There are dangerous animals in my room! They're going to kill me! Come quickly!'

The friend had the same dream three times.

The third time, the man in the farmhouse cried, 'It's too late! I'm already dead! They've killed me and hidden my body. Go to the west gate of the town. You'll find my body there.'

So the friend went to the west gate, and there he found the body.

◆

Chaunticleer said, 'You see, dreams have meanings. Now, I'll tell you another story.'

This was his second story.

◆

Two men wanted to sail across the sea, but they had to wait for the right wind.

They went to stay in a city near the sea, and decided to sail early the next day. They went to bed in the same room. They were happy that they could start their journey soon.

But in the night one of the men dreamed that he saw a man in their room. This man said to him, 'If you sail tomorrow, you'll die. Stay here, in the city, for one more day. Then you'll be safe.'

The man woke up and told his friend the story, but his friend laughed at him. He didn't believe that the dream was true.

'The wind's right today,' he said. 'You stay here if you want to wait. I'm leaving. Dreams mean nothing! Goodbye!'

He walked away and the man never saw his friend again. The ship sailed onto some rocks, and all the men in it were killed.

◆

Then Chaunticleer told Pertelote his third story. It was about the King of Mercia's son.

This little boy was only seven years old. He dreamed that he was in great danger. He told a kind woman about his dream but she didn't believe him. Nobody believed his dream.

A few days later, the king's sister killed the little boy.

◆

Chaunticleer finished his stories and said, 'My dear Pertelote, I feel better now. I'm not frightened. Let's fly down to the garden.'

The cock and his wife both flew down from the roof and Chaunticleer called all his hens to him. He felt like a king and he wasn't afraid.

It was a beautiful morning. When Chaunticleer sang, his voice sounded happy and strong. He happily told the world what time it was.

'Madam Pertelote,' he said, 'listen to the birds. They sound wonderful! And look at the flowers. They look lovely after their long winter's sleep. My love, my heart is full of happiness.'

But then a terrible thing happened.

A fox lived in the little wood near the old woman's house. He came into the garden during the night and hid quietly behind the trees until it was midday. 'That's the best time to catch poor Chaunticleer,' he thought to himself.

◆

'Oh, Chaunticleer,' the nun's priest said, 'it was a bad day for you! You came down from your safe roof into the dangerous garden! You tried to forget your dream – but it was true!

'It was a mistake for Chaunticleer to listen to his wife. Women are often wrong. But I'm a nun's priest, so I mustn't say too much against women!'

◆

Pertelote was sitting happily in the sun with all her sisters round her. Chaunticleer stood near them, singing loudly.

Then the cock heard a noise and turned quickly. There was the fox! He stopped singing immediately. He felt very, very frightened.

'Dear sir,' said the fox, 'why have you stopped singing? I'm your friend. I don't want to hurt you. You sing beautifully, like your mother and father. They've both been to my house. They were very kind to come. I was very happy to have them there.

'I've never heard anyone sing like your father on that morning. He shut his eyes and stood up tall. Now, please sir, can you sing for me like your father?'

Chaunticleer was very pleased to hear these words. He didn't understand the fox's true meaning. So he stood up tall, shut his eyes, and began to sing.

The fox suddenly caught Chaunticleer and threw him on his back. Then he ran with him towards the wood.

The hens saw the fox and made a terrible noise. Pertelote made the loudest noise. The old woman and her two daughters ran out of their house when they heard her.

'Fox! Fox!' they cried out, and ran into the wood. The seven hens followed them, then the old woman's three dogs, and the other farm animals. People ran out of their houses and threw things at the fox.

The women shouted, 'Fox! Fox!' The hens ran – 'Cluck!

Cluck!' The dogs ran – 'Woof! Woof!' Everyone followed the fox and poor Chaunticleer.

◆

'Now, good people,' said the nun's priest, 'you must listen to the end of my story. Then you'll learn something.'

◆

The fox ran deeper and deeper into the wood with Chaunticleer in his mouth. When he stopped for a rest, the cock spoke to him.

'Sir Fox, you must turn round and speak to those stupid people. Say to them, "Go back home! I've reached the wood now and I'm going to eat this cock. You can't do anything about it, so stop making that noise. Go home!"'

'That's a good idea,' answered the fox.

Of course, when the fox opened his mouth to speak, he dropped Chaunticleer. The cock quickly flew up into a high tree.

'Oh, dear Sir Chaunticleer,' said the fox, as he looked up didn't want to frighten you. I didn't really want to eat you. C⸱ down, and talk to me.'

'No,' shouted Chaunticleer, 'I'm not coming down. I've bⴹⴹ very stupid but now I understand you!'

'Ah!' replied the fox. 'I was the stupid one. I spoke when you were in my mouth. I must learn to keep my mouth shut.'

◆

'So,' said the nun's priest, 'don't believe everything that people say to you in this world. My story isn't just a simple one about a fox, a cock and seven hens. It can teach you important things. You can learn from it.'

'Thank you,' said the pilgrims. 'Thank you, Sir Priest, for a very good story.'

ACTIVITIES

The Prologue and The Knight's Tale

Before you read

1 Find Canterbury on a map of England. How far is it from London? How long does it take to get there, do you think? How long did it take on horseback?

2 Look at the picture on page 8. What kind of story do you think *The Knight's Tale* is?

3 Find these words in your dictionary. They are all in the story.

   duke inn pilgrim poison temple tower

   Which one is:

   a a religious place?

   b a religious traveller?

   c a strong tall building?

   d an important man?

   e a place with food, drink and rooms?

   f a way of killing someone?

4 How are these different? Check the words in your dictionary.

   a a *saint* and *God*

   b a *tale* and a *prologue*

   c a *lord* and a *servant*

   Now write three sentences with these words.

After you read

5 In the *Prologue*:

   a Why did pilgrims want to travel to Canterbury?

   b Where do the pilgrims in Chaucer's story meet?

   c Who wants the pilgrims to tell stories? Why?

6 Are Palamon and Arcite friends at the beginning, middle and end of *The Knight's Tale*? Why do their feelings change?

The Clerk's Tale, The Wife of Bath's Tale, and The Pardoner's Tale

Before you read

7 Look at the pictures in these stories. In which story:

    a do some stupid young men look for Death?

    b does a beautiful young wife lose her children?

    c does a knight marry an ugly old woman?

8 Find the word *fairy* in your dictionary. Do you know a story about fairies? Tell another student.

After you read

9 Who:

    a finds the answer to a difficult question?

    b tests his wife's love for him?

    c drinks poison and dies slowly?

    Which story is each person in?

10 Work with another student. Have two conversations.

    a *Student A:* You are Griselda in *The Clerk's Tale*. Walter has found a new wife and you have returned home to your father. Tell Janicula about your life with Walter.

        Student B: You are Janicula. Ask Griselda how she feels about Walter now. Is she sad about her children?

    b *Student A:* You are the old woman who is married to the knight in *The Wife of Bath's Tale*. Tell the knight the wise things you know.

        Student B: You are the knight. Ask the old woman how she knows these things.

The Franklin's Tale, The Friar's Tale, and The Nun's Priest's Tale

Before you read

11 Choose a picture from one of these stories. What do you think the story is about? Does it have a happy or a sad ending?

12 Find these words in your dictionary.

bailiff cock devil fox hell hen magic

Now put the words into this table:

Bird	Animal	Person	Place

Which words do not go into the table?

After you read

13 Who says these words? In which story? What are they talking about?
  a 'I always loved my husband!'
  b 'A promise is a promise, my dear.'
  c 'I must learn to keep my mouth shut.'

14 Is it always right to keep a promise? Why/why not? Have you ever broken an important promise?

15 In your opinion, do some dreams come true? Have you ever had a dream that came true? Tell another student about it.

Writing

16 You are the fat man who owns the Tabard Inn. You have to judge which story is best. Choose one of the stories. Why is it better than the others?

17 List the people who are happy at the end of the stories. Do you think the ending is right for each of these people? Why/why not?

18 Who do you like most in the stories? And who do you like least? Why?

19 Some of the stories teach us lessons. Write about the lessons in *The Clerk's Tale*, *The Friars's Tale* and *The Nun's Priest's Tale*.

Answers for the Activities in this book are available from your local office or alternatively write to: Penguin Readers Marketing Department, Pearson Education, Edinburgh Gate, Harlow, Essex CM20 2JE.